Nevrospastos (The Puppet)

Sameer S Nilatkar

Presentation by *BookLeaf Publishing*

Web: www.bookleafpub.com

E-mail: info@bookleafpub.com

ISBN: 9789360947279

First edition 2024

ACKNOWLEDGEMENT

Thank you Amruta for pulling the strings (pun intended). Without you, this book would not have seen the light of the day.

I'm Marionette

Let me tell you how much I hate being
controlled by strings
The being who pulls me is unaware of things
Why should I cry when I want to smile
Why should I dance
When I want to rest a while
My arms go stiff and my fingers numb.

Knees ache and foot swollen
For you, I shall muster all the strength
And try to express myself with eyes
But you know, they are painted with your lies
You point me towards the East, West, North and
South
Well, you have even sealed my mouth

Never disclosed to me who my parents are
Only characters who are afar
There are times when I wish to break free
Run away to the woods and hug a tree
I did manage to escape from your clutches
Hiding amongst the witches and the granny who
stitches
Finally reaching the woods
I hugged a tree and cried my heart out
The witch whispered to me
This is the same tree that carved you out.

Lovers Longing

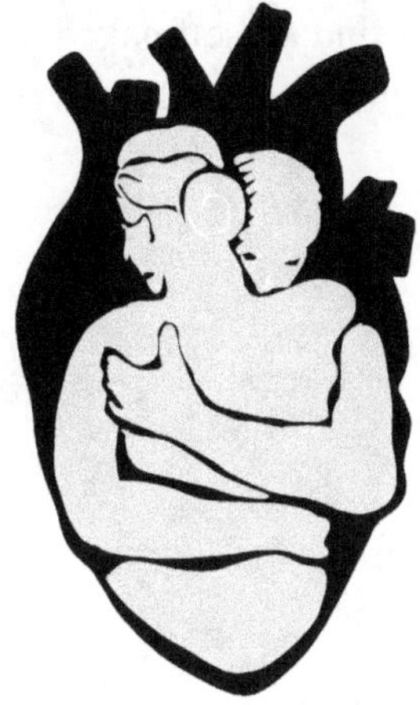

Lovers longing
Longing through the dark, waiting for the
morning hue.
Forever the thought that you shall walk in my
life.
Oh this strife, the mind and body are always
going astride.
When will you come, to play on my chest,
running your fingers, on my vest.
The touch that I'm longing for that shall send
ripples afar.
Waiting endlessly through the pitch dark, to the
first light, and the whole world is ajar.
I see many a familiar grin, but not the one who
is akin.

Like a weary traveler, looking for that glance, a
perfect moment, forever in trance.
Seeking you, I find myself naked, joyful enough
for another night, yield to this lover's
plight.

Fruit of Labour

No, you can't be the fruit of labor
For I have toiled, so much and so far
I could see the pink flowers, up high
The path upward looks precipitous
I struggled a bit, gathered up
Looking back, the path I came,
Was hazardous, yet I never looked back,
No, you can't be the fruit of labor
For the earth laughs in flowers
Fruits are rooted in the ground.

Colors of Noise

As I entered a near-empty room
My eyes hovered for a sight of you
Sitting relaxed on the venerable couch
With a glass of rum in one hand
And the Marlboro in another
But that was not the case this time
And you were gone
Before entering my life
Now I could hear the humming of the fan
I remember the day we went to your farmhouse
It was a bright sunny day
With cold winds and blue skies
Your bike went dry on the empty highway
I slept on your shoulder
With the sound of tyres kissing the road

My eyes ran wet, I struggled to collect the tears
Briskly went towards the tap
Thought of washing my face
Water dispensed pokily
It took me back again
On the day it was light rain
We went for an ice-cream
Yours was chocolate and I preferred a
butterscotch
Hand in hand, we took a walk down the river
The brutal wind made your cheeks shiver
I hate to admit that every oise reminds me, you
are near

It's hardly about ten minutes in this room
I can hear a frightening thunder
I pick up myself and make my way to the door
Hastily running down the stairs
My high heels made noise like a waterfall
Reminds me of our vacation in Costa Rica
How we spent the night in a secret cave
At the Diamante Waterfall

I descend the stairs and arrive at the lobby
Open the ornate door
It's raining heavily and your thoughts haunting
eerily
I hate to admit that every noise reminds me, you
are near.

Kebab

The sight of a chargrilled chunk of meat
And the voracious eater comes alive
He is gluttonous to the extent of ordering a
whole platter
All by himself, along with some wine
For he has pretty much a carnassial tooth
Tearing apart the soft flesh
And he begins to masticate
Closing his eyes, he chews on
Not only the food but also the thoughts
Such a glutton he is
Admiring the light red color of the meat
Like a subterranean fire in the ocean
And how the aroma of the burn
Abruptly pulls him towards the Kebabforush
For him the sight is angelic

Of skewers lined up on a pit like a scabbard
The dripping of oil mixed with the meat juice
And the charcoal comes alive
With a myriad of colors
For him, it is like the parched land
Has received its first drop of rain
To a glutton, the aroma is pompous
That determines the acceptance
Whether the meat is medium or well-done
He wishes to gorge forever
Till the last of the Shish is cleaned up
Now he has had his bellyful
He straddles his way on the busy bazaar street
A few meters away
Another sight of a chargrilled chunk of meat
And the voracious eater comes alive...

Oxytocin

A while ago, we were strangers at the Bar
Sitting across the counter on a high bar stool
You, in the little black dress
Rhythm Divine by Enrique played in a loop
The Chopard on your wrist, the Happy
Diamonds
The diffused light evenly lit your face

Our eyes met and whispered cheers
The glasses clink and a mischievous blink
Stealing you from the enchanted space
We drive away towards the desert
A place of great stillness
You and I being the only constant

Driving in the arid landscape
I left my stress far behind
We hopped on a motel
With neon light and not a soul in sight
Goodnight chocolate next to the pillow
And we tucked ourselves in bed

We cuddled amidst the soft sheets
Is it the love hormone?
That pea-like structure beneath the
hypothalamus
Which brought us together
Or is it the estrogen that is related to the cuddle
hormone?
Well, it drove away our stress and anxiety
Eyes were moist, yet the eyelids felt buoyant
It was absolute bliss
Never felt like this ever before
This definitely must be, what they call...
Oxytocin.

On my Journal

Random thoughts and connecting the dots
Numerous To-do lists and clenched fists
Now and then in cursive
And also quite abusive
Depending upon mood
The pen does sometimes brood
Most weekdays are filled with flowcharts
And weekends are casual matters of the heart
Recording events of my life
Or matters of personal strife
Getting thoughts on paper
And delve into me deeper
This is an exercise to get organized
Discover oneself and be energized
It does offer a memory boost
For positive ideas perched on a roost

Often I ponder
When time is slender
What do I call my journal
Few have a Bullet Journal
A few call it an Idea or Gratitude Journal
Mine is always in plain sight
That gives me valuable insight
What should I keep its name
Or should I simply call it the time frame

Black Coffee

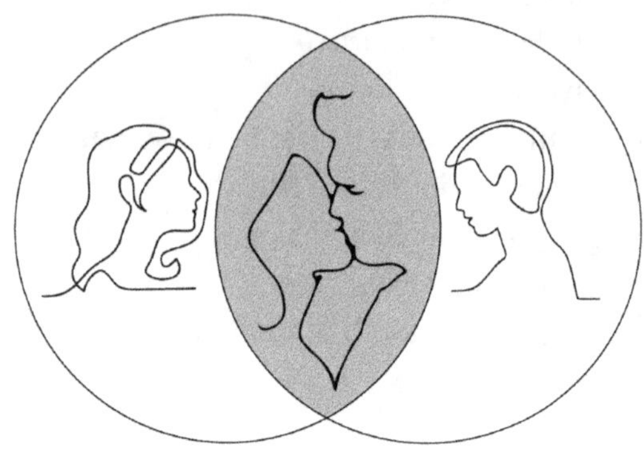

I'm glad, I finally left you ...
Sitting in this cozy swing chair
Of what once belonged to you
Sipping my poison
My favorite black coffee
In the chipped mug you despised me for
Our relationship, like coffee
Was dark, bitter and acidic
When we first met
I was unroasted, like a green bean
You steeped me in your love
Like the beans steeped in hot water
Over time, our relationship changed
To myriad colors
From beige to brown and finally black
As time passed by, I was like a qahwah
The dark one
And now, you have cleansed me

Like the coffee plantation which cleanses the
Rainforest
Making it parched
The bright memory spots
Still afresh in me
Like the coffee leaf, I was vibrant and glossy
You said I was luscious
Like the fragrant white flower of the coffee plant
We met and I rejoiced
Like the seed planted in the rainy season
Gradually you infected me
Like a fungal pathogen
For you thought, I'm fit to be fed to worms
You plucked the relationship
At the peak of ripeness
Yes, you changed my life
Just like the coffee bean
Roasted me, physically and chemically
I wasn't the same woman, emotionally
Like a good coffee
I tend to absorb
The surroundings, and matters close to your
heart
You brought the seed in me to life
By adding water
Yet, finally, I lost my color
And you served me... iced.

The Sleep

I crash into bed
Gazing towards the ceiling fan
Random thoughts run across
Like a PowerPoint slide-show
Some are fun and some somber
While some are flashes of lights
Strung on a Gulmohar tree
I try to catch on to the most absorbing
And it makes a hasty retreat
Trying to recollect
What was that
Another thought
Pounces upon
I'm not gonna let this one slip away
Might as well sleep through the day

A burst of colors
And golden blobs
Beyond the curtain
Someone sobs
As I enter paradoxical sleep
This thought runs deep
I managed to get a hold
And take a peep
It is me who is sobbing
The alarm kicks-in
It is 7 am
Eyes wide awake
Now I think
It is me who is blabbing

Sin City

Old fella has been around for many years
The city, that brought him joy and tears
Saw his beard grow from anagen to catagen and
now glitter
Yes, not so long ago
He was a clean-shaven man
Trying to climb the corporate ladder
He reminiscences about his bachelor days
When he came to the city of dreams
A bag in hand and jolly good ice cream
Soon he lands a job
And a decent accommodation
Gets blended into the city's commotion
Those Wednesday nights
And tipsy bar fights
Picking up girls
And drive through the city lights

One fine day, he finds the girl of his dreams
It was love like a ray of sunbeam
He switches his jobs
And climbs up the ladder
Those Wednesday nights
Now fill up the bladder
Soon he gets married
And has two kids
Success in life makes him take big bids
The lure of a good life
Amidst personal strife
Pulled and kneaded like a dough
Seeds of discomfort sow
He straddles through the murky waters of life
Now he is all alone
In the city of dreams
He is a bearded man
Trying to hang on the ladder
With nothing but his proud glitter

The Silly Lily

I'm a Lily
Curvaceous and herbaceous
Arising out of a bulb
A real beauty with a large prominent flower
Enjoying the best, being a perennial
Buried deep in the ground before I blossom
Emimiting analogous colors
In shades of Orange, Red, Purple, Pink
And sometimes, White and Yellow
Isn't it silly that real beauty does have
Spots and strokes
Where the gentle hand pokes
I flower in late spring or summer
Some say, I'm a funnel shape
And some, a Turk cap or Trumpet Lily
I do show moods in warm weather

A celebrity I am, mentioned in the Song of
Solomon
As a symbol of virginal innocence
And decorate your home, as a patio plant
Isn't it silly, that I gorge on a porous, loamy soil
Yet sometimes, I'm a toxic recoil
I'm edible and a trusted vegetable
Made into a soup and often stir-fried
In case your thoughts are clamoring
I'm also used as a flavoring agent
Isn't it silly, that I portray love, ardor and
affection
And also the soul of the deceased
Besides being an Honor of the Royalty.

The Sunday Ride

Each Sunday is a blessing in guise
Man, machine and the gorgeous sunrise
It is dawn and my palms itchy
To kiss the leather gloves
Start the bike and search for hidden troves
There is a lakeside, the offbeat track
There is a highway and a place where hills crack
For a nomad biker, there's no fixed path
For he feels joyous in a dust bath
The rubber on the road, shedding tears
Is music to his ears
He is a jolly bloke
Who enjoys the exhaust smoke

Wearing his biker's jacket
He feels knighted
The formal and informal are not his type
For him, the attire is a hype
Wind, water and heat in his stride
And ceaseless wilderness by the side
The machine guzzling gallons of fuel
Both enjoy the eccentric duel
He wishes that every Monday could have been a
Sunday
Cause each Sunday is a blessing in guise
Man, machine and the gorgeous sunrise.

A Hoggers Breakfast

Nothing escapes the gut
Why settle for the breakfast sausage
When you have the bratwurst and chorizo
With a helping of bacon slices
Seared well in its juices
Then there's charcuterie
A humongous combo of pate, salami and cheese
I pick them up with grubby hands
Wash it down with orange juice
The egg station looks enticing
I rush towards the melee
And give a shout-out
Two sunny-side-up please
I order the grumpy chef

For he's had a long night before he calls it a day
Thankfully the eggs come my way
Toasted multigrain bread
Is rolled up and dipped in the yolk
A sight to behold
Like a fresh lava flow
There are preserves too
Margarine, butter and jam
They all shall go down my intestinal dam
Amidst the chitter chatter
My lavished attention
Goes towards the fruit platter
Melons, pears and grapes
A couple of bananas form a scatter
The Chef De Cuisine comes across
With a dessert cart
Sitting on its top is an artisanal bread art
Two Danish pastries are picked up
And a black coffee gobbled up.

The Kind Man

Tough times call tough men
I was never that man
Raised with great affection
I was that man who craved affection
One fine day
I was left alone
Brothers, sisters and friends
All remained bygone
A sudden surge of motivation came by
The calf I tended to
Sang me a lullaby
Quickly I rose to my feet
To face the world
And its fleet
Broken, beaten and smothered
By the very people

For whom I bothered
Revenge was on my mind
I set out to relinquish
One by one the bygones were gathered
As I was about to strike by
I became withered
I was never that man
I had great affection

Candlelight Dinner

We were so much in love
Hand in hand forever
I took you out for a candlelight dinner
You wore a chic cocktail gown
The beachside setting
And a perfect evening
The candles and string lights
The warm glow on your face
Exotic cocktails in sunset color
Followed by oysters and champagne
The sweet scent of the aroma candle
Set up the romantic mood
The whipped cream and berries
Was the perfect dessert
I wanted to slip in the diamond ring

And make you mine forever
But you, you were never ready
For commitment
I finished you with the same knife and fork
There was blood on the plate
And mind over matter.

An Odd Invite

As a frequent rider
I often venture into the uncharted path
One sunny afternoon
The heat sears my bomber jacket
What worse could happen
Than a flat tyre
On the lone highway
Not a single soul in sight
To heed my plight
For a while
Dragging the bike along
I break out in a sweat
Few meters ahead
I see a mirage
It feels soothing

To view nature's collage
I'm a mile down now
And spot an old fella
With a withered face
I say hello
Uneasiness vanishes without a trace
Smoking a joint
He comes to the point
Help is a few miles ahead
His hut is nearby
I follow him
Through the bushes
A piping hot cuppa tea
Made with jaggery
By far, the best I had
In an earthenware cup
And the company of his feline kitten
Charged up now
I'm ready for a few miles ahead
I offer him a hundred rupee note
For his hospitality
He refuses
And teaches me a lesson about humanity.

The Couple

A coffee shop named Love
A youngish boy
Came by, with a girl whom he called Dove
The boy, in a white tee and black denim
The girl, in denim slims
They order a frappe and blueberry cheesecake
And wide grins their time would take
The quaint little corner table
Should be sufficient for their fable
Eye to eye, they discuss about vanity
And the next-door girl
Who questioned their sanity.

The Devil's Ice-cream

I often see this as a tempter of humankind
Such a wonderful colloidal emulsion,
With a burst of colors
Of every imagination,
I'm however particularly attracted
To the strawberry red
It is closest to what a devil has in bed,
For it is the ultimate dessert
To wash down one's Epicurean sins,
Those who don't go to heaven
Are whisked here in hell,
The sweetness liberates you
In the belly, it flows gracefully
As the spice makes way for the dessert,

I once had a beautiful mortal
Tender she was
Like the scoops delicately balanced on a Dixie
Cup,
That thought exalted my appetite
Cleaved apart her belly
An ocean of red outpoured,
Her inanimate eyes
Had a cherry-like shine,
A nebulous night I cherished
For a long, I had wished
To relish a Sundae,
The corridors of Hell
Are served with frozen sin.

Cryptic

Your message was cryptic last night
It was mysterious and appeared like a flashlight
Hard for me to understand
What should be my next stand
Then again, another text
And you thought, why make it obscure
Let's catch up for drinks and gulp some absinthe
I said that would be better
Instead of going labyrinth
We met at a fine dining, whose name was
Mysterious
The setting of the place seemed ambiguous
Unknowingly, I uttered a few words confusing
You polished them further and made them
mystifying
How we got along is puzzling
And for the patrons watching us
It seemed perplexing

What transpired between us was arcane
For the dining house staff
It was pretty mundane
Round of drinks flowed freely
And we spoke further abstrusely
We thought, let's have some food
And order what's popular
Where the menu seems oracular
We finally settled for a falafel
To whet our appetites garble
The thought of love was hazy
And we were inherently fuzzy
There was no point
Being in love and still being fathomless
Instead, let's be cryptic
And be clueless...

The Tribal Girl

The scorching sun
Reflecting upon your silver earrings
Bending and illuminating
Those amulets and necklace
A brief smirk
Highlights your life in isolation
The sunken eyes
That speaks of the silent majority
The strong jawline
That defies prejudice
Spindly lips
Speaking of your comfort in solitude
The weather-beaten face
Malleable by toiling in the fields
Dusky complexion

That conforms to your love of animism
Dusk falls watching your serpentine dance
The culture keeper of the clan
Is wedded for a price
She has all it takes
Yet being looked upon
As a bird of passage.

The Drink

After all the modifications of the mind have
dwindled
The throat is parched by dusk,
I sit back relaxed
At a bog-standard bar,
Having my steady whiskey
Watching a few drunk patrons
Getting frisky,
The drink alone is capable of giving me
liberation
I'm a seeker of peace,
The first sip gave me a superior consciousness
For the drink, I'm a refuge seeker
And the drinker feeds on its blissful nature,
What a delight it is, to have that one drink
And enfold oneself in relaxing sleep,
Each sip permeates into the veins
And the drinker manifests in varied forms

A few drinks down and you are in disposition,
The urban fellow, dwells in the middle
Pulled by the irresistible power
And not limited by time,
Each drink has an immortal bliss
More potent than a cakey kiss,
As I sit back and look at the drink
A water of cosmic dissolution
I could perceive that every problem has a
solution.

Granny's Pickle

The taste still lingers on my tongue
Each papilla drenched
In acid and mustard oil
And those galactic ceramic jars
That stored these memories
For years together
Occupying the top shelf on the kitchen rack
The aroma, spreading long
Towards the verandah
Where another batch of cut raw mangoes
Were being dried
Alongside, lemon pickle
Was also being tried
Balancing the flavor
The Yin and Yang,
Years later
I became a Chef
I said, let me try my hand at recreating

Granny's awesome pickle
In went all the ingredients
And the magic masalas
With hot mustard oil
Stored it in similar ceramic jars
And waited for that enticing aroma
Days and months passed by
Yet all I could sense was the
Pungent smoky hell
A year passed by
And the pickle was untouched
It was my twenty-seventh birthday
And I said, let's open the pickle jar
There goes the index finger
Taking a springboard dive
The dark amber color
Came out exceedingly well,
I grinned, and thought, I hit the bullseye
Popped it on my tongue
It was an utter disappointment
The taste was not the same
I feel, my efforts were lame.